CELLULOID SALUTATIONS

CELLULOID SALUTATIONS

(AN OXYMORONIC ODE TO LESLIE SCALAPINO)

OR: A POEM FOR THE EMPTINESS IN ANIMAL'S BELLY

ELIZABETH BLOCK

BLAZEVOX[BOOKS]
Buffalo, New York

CELLULOID SALUTATIONS
by Elizabeth Block

Copyright © 2014

Published by BlazeVOX [books]

All rights reserved. No part of this book may be reproduced without
the publisher's written permission, except for brief quotations in reviews.

Printed in the United States of America

Interior design and typesetting by Geoffrey Gatza
Cover image: Amanda Hughen, *Electroembryonic*, acrylic paint, ink, and pencil on mylar, 6x6 inches, 2009

First Edition
ISBN: 978-1-60964-122-1
Library of Congress Control Number: 2013945255

BlazeVOX [books]
131 Euclid Ave
Kenmore, NY 14217

Editor@blazevox.org

publisher of weird little books

BlazeVOX [books]

blazevox.org

21 20 19 18 17 16 15 14 13 12 01 02 03 04 05 06 07 08 09 10

BlazeVOX

"There are three times—a present of things past, a present of things present, and a present of things future." For these three do exist in the mind, and I do not see them anywhere else: the present time of things past is memory; the present time of things present is sight; the present time of things future is expectation. If we are allowed to use words in this way, then I see that there are three times and I admit that there are."

—St. A, from *the Confessions of St. Augustine*

"Prose is a house, poetry a man in flames running quite fast through it."

—Anne Carson, *red doc>*

"(For with all her knowledge of history, Alice had no very clear notion how long ago anything happened)"

—Lewis Carroll, *Alice in Wonderland*

This book is for my husband and my daughter

Table of Contents:

N.B.:

Text Sources:

Virginia Woolf, *To the Lighthouse* (1927) and *On Being Ill* (1930)
Sir Thomas de Quincey, *Confessions of an Opium Eater* (1821)
Johanna Drucker, *Intimations of Immateriality* (2002)
Edmund Parish, *Hallucinations and Illusions* (1897) (Out of Print)
Stephen Levine, *Gradual Awakenings*
William Faulker, *Light in August* (1932)
And, of course, Leslie Scalapino's poem, *Instead of Animal* (1978) and philosophy of poetry, in general, with utmost respect for her contributions to the field of poetics

These text sources intermingle with my own writing, and generally not as direct quotes. Rather, I re-work the text sources into what I perceive to be dyslexic language patterns, and I randomly select words that stand out to me and (without adherence to cause and effect) co-mingle them. When I do quote authors verbatim, I announce quotes.

Excerpts of this manuscript (individual poems) have been previously published in/on:

Chain 15
Documents Between
Just Pretent Everything is OK: Evri Kwong Art Exhibition (funded by the Lannan Foundation)
Strewnpackedcinderwhateverlight (the film by Elizabeth Block; Distributed by Canyon Cinema)
Make Haste, Slowly, (the film by Elizabeth Block; Distributed by Canyon Cinema)
Santa Fe Art Institute, *Art in Public Transit* (Poetry)
NON/FICTIONS, Canyon Cinemazine, Issue No.2 Summer 2013

CELLULOID SALUTATIONS

I: Make Haste, Slowly

Make Haste, Slowly

After night

night, winter and summer storms of torment, the like-arrow stillness of weather fine, their
court, without, held interference. Had (listening there any been to listen one), the, from
rooms upper empty, the only house chaos gigantic lighting streaked with have, could, heard,
been tossing and tumbling: the wind as the waves themselves disported, amorphous,

like the bulks whose leviathans are brows pierced by light no reason of; mounted and on one
another top and plunged, lunged darkness in the daylight or (night for day and, month year
and shapelessly together ran) in games idiot, it, until seemed if as universe—the battling—
were tumbling confusion, in brute want and lust

itself aimlessly by.

The shadows,

only of trees. The flourishing wind in obeisance made the wall, on, for, and darkened moment in the pool, which reflected and suspected light itself. Birds, or flying a made spot soft, slowly flutter, across floor bedroom of night dreams fumbling— mumble of what—left their heads across the way.

To the going, light, what but does one send?
Alone, green-gray, faltering the house, light the wall on opposite. The places empty. Were such parts of the somehow, fan.

But them together, bring.

She wants to whirl

                                                            out of nowhere

                                                    she gets up, it is dark.

The buzzing of the little head she thought she knew,
she thought maybe it was another day not to begin, but to sing,
she wanted it out of her mouth, the taste waiting into the, who is it that calls her

perhaps nobody can tell you about the dizzy dance; she moves through layers of noise, what
kind of noise, we don't know yet, the person bad that her took away is not now dead, but in
her head, she tells that one is out of sight,

now mind out of

    too.

It-was-it tentative, gradual, one as goes a shelving down beach sea into deepening, with and
knowledge lying dangers of—that path? For the lozenges, often-times pulmonary relief,
efficacy on affectations, opium within contained, disavowing clamorously an alliance,
suspicious.

Back to the ultraviolet burst, the lighthouse retrieved, centrifuge
a tittle.

(Not present, no)

It-was-it tentative, gradual, one as goes a shelving down beach sea into deepening, with and knowledge lying dangers of—that path? For the lozenges, oftentimes pulmonary relief, efficacy on affectations, opium within contained, disavowing clamorously an

alliance, suspicious.

Procrastination dreadful.

Mad, idiosyncratic in ways, they go. Lurching, and through cloudbanks, high flying and ether.
But inconstant colors ravishing.
Aspiration—fitful, fragmented—funny. Respiration. Ice across crystal fields.

Moon me to the fly.

Moon pallid,
wheel.

Moon pallid,
wheel.

Animal Animal Animal
Forgive me
You came at me, staggering,

Projective, wailing attack

My breasts aflame
Sucking
Pumping
Sucking
Pumping my way out of this

The tear of *this is my birth story* what is yours?

I mean, I cannot pump my way out of this
And time has passed
Animal

Not just now, forever, and yesterday, and tomorrow
This *is* my birth story
Not the placenta I dragged behind

Moon me to the fly.

II: Like Automatic

Seeing Automatic (like Automatic Writing)

1.

Sounds inarticulate
recognizable without
uttered vigorously meaning rigorous
vociferation as discern
objectively ecstatic or
Tongues
in speaking; the utterance-when feeble
perception
subjective noise
"confused"
voices many same time of talking
same made up

Automatic in action, the, of, apparatus-seeing muscular.

2.

The hand same the sentence or word again and over over (writing-mirror, seeing, etc.,
anagrams).

Perception subjective again: sentence the same or over-heard, e.g.,

"eat, do not"
or strange words, non-dictionariable words: grak-lolch, rorrim.

3.

Perception again
subjective
"strange" voices I'm hearing
you hear
"made are thoughts up for me" (develops this case out of sometimes former the)
perception
objective/not
prophecy sonambulate

Often long the write hands, complicated, the to consciousness, sublime
belonging.

4.

: perception, the subject:
thinking double audible thinking
attacks of chattering chit chat
spasms-mime-y

coordinated

The write hands consciously what the thinking is person, but person the not does
intention write the influence.

5.

voices directed, pleasure

Writes the hand (automatically), the train conscious of thought, the of, part on the
communication influences place where the:

Instinct
Never waiting to see
A fancy neighborhood
Dog
Mean

Mauls a 13 year old girl
My 1 year-old
A witness

Trapped in the car

She never forgets the past

Gone:

Are we not?

On Being Un-

So in there, I wait

The unless American happier
Making words new than in old
Disposition

Outspoken childish
Illness in
Blurted truths out
Respected conceals health
Illusions
Jerks wrist
Excursions unprofitable
Beggar's old misery of hieroglyphic

Roof thatch the men
Flowers disdainful
No pains at conceal
To nature
Leave will the world heat
The will to go sun out
Surface of irregularity
Ancient boundary

Grak-lolch
She spanks and takes
The whole this and that
My edge

The garden of . . .

rock under sky   un oubli

no one knows

Illness of the Text

Public the

Raptures

Monster its tapers

With beat rapid

Influenza

Devoted novel to

Plot lacked

Love of disguise

Ears pricked

Coined to force

Words

Pure lump

Of sound

Babel

New brand idea

Drops end out

Happier

In the before never

Disposed

Constitutes what

The text

Nature of?

Information scheme

Threads, stacks, rhizomes

Linked

Yesterday you touched me

Where I didn't want you to.

Message actual

What are you doing here?

I don't know.

You know, of course you know.

Level basic, let's start

The letter

Bound between

Text and storage

From visual graphic

Form

As if you wanted

To rip off my clothes,

and for a moment I wanted you to.

Missed you:::

There—

Illness, because

a language requires new

go we here alone

solitude profers

will I make up a new language?

Intensely physical

Like a glass of pane

Experience transmitter

Electric signal

Cinema of cloud-scapes

The shiver

The mouth

More obscene

Taste liquid sweet

Dialects of sweet talk

Purposes specialized

Sense related to form

An archived interrogation

Dropped type

Document

Un-libraried

By an obsolescence

Seeming utilitarian

Grown

Out of soiled organic

Herbs stalk me

Now

I want to eat

the Mediterranean sea

It has disappeared
Apparently
But not entirely so
If you are rich

A love of the chemicals
Majestic
I know you

interventions

a sheet is a plain of glass
body
which though soul the
straight looks clear
too many people watch the beheading
on the infrared representation

one for save two
passions
desire:/greed:/
non-existent
none-null
negligible

always
intervenes the physical world
sharpens and blunts

I thought I knew that writing would clear things up
Now pictures travel all around my tail

Noble plans

Smithereens itself to smashes

Optical Character Recognition

Hallucinatoria Paranoia

Insulting taunting
Voices
Deceptions-sense
Letterforms in the display
Confound elasticity this requirement
Reductive
Identity algorithmic
Reduction

Unseen speakers words
Let
Fall
Long frequently
Persistent
Is this the whole of all stay with me before I look somewhere else
Perception common-sense
Letters seem
Essential to have a form
Beclouding dreamlike of intellect opinions
Amentia
Color bleeds around the edges of my said
Mind
You cannot come into the wild those poppies they really get to me as if nature blurred me
out of the possibilities
We tried to get there every day
walked on head
Objects are scalable letter fonts

They do not
simple memory to correspond
Concussion molecular
Glass-magnifying all look-though

"if a letter were in fact" algorithmically fundamental
"its shape and distinctive graphical feature"
prescribed
could be

The sprockets
Cascade
Squares
Jam
The projector

Light again
I've lost you

                              as variations
                         single on a formula

come again take
look for the weeds underneath the sea
like you know how it goes things don't get up

order natural of the way we seem to see
reversed as if—
you know
recumbent, lying
ears pricked for the stairs ascended
creaking
twitch
twiddle-daddle
un-ending whole changes process of delirium
if as to wait say and more

every time I thought it would go that way

it stopped
and turned around to make me not
greelitarutalimont
"Mrs. Jones catches her train."
Where I sat and legs frozen
"Mr. Smith mends his motor."
Can you only
Stare into the bolt some more
Stalk the everyday that breaks down

She would not know that she couldn't speak
Of things she could not talk and delirious you are my old nightgown

Holding me inside a silk
Waist

The matter never gets figured out we want it to we think all day long on it until the pitter
patter of undying sequential thoughts in my head attempt to fell a new one that wants to
apprehend phenomena available only in the order natural of twigs and babies who you are you
fold yourself inside little leaves the bugs get in there they twirl inside the comprehension the
favorable islands of entrapment where interminable asterisks help you decide you better leave
before tonight as the whirling dust climbs up to the surface of the ill—lit moon, spinning
dervish of a camera lens takes it up there with you and that is all that carries it past my sighs
oh you just want to give it all away before you have but one last ream of paper to tell it on the
tree sap come drip slide as we walk into the gloaming nigh high where we romance have it
always looking things down the road, is it mine is it mine and how you assert yourself.

I'm not there

She was not there

So in the morning patter
The dizzelectiforoporous
Noun

Wherefore the dawn hits the something I swore this swoon easier than she knew before she
Commits\

Words erase the things they thought they were saying to you like how we ignored you because
we didn't want them to know how great you were
We ignored you
Because human beings just want to

Interference is the wonderful

And we mixed you to go not there
In this
Stray verb
Swerve

You can think this is the most gone over flatly gone through the high strung thing that worlds
ring a ding ding in the finger head
She walks away

And purple indecision thinks it outsmarts every little go to it baby boy go to it get your little
dingy ding

Swing

Garupswiddleforth

Sweet little oyster fiddle frog

You and so what kinda true
I think I'll tweak eat too

nothing

Spring recumbent

Want to say that music is not linguistic
Is weight
Senses clamped on something you never thought you knew
Flings life itself the wave
Indefatigably out
So even sheeted the earth whole
Undulation, some slippery
Irregularity will mark the surface
An ancient garden boundary
There
Starlight, flower will rose
Burn will crocus
Life of hook will
In us still
Must we wriggle?

"But I beneath a rougher sea"

Was leaning
The water sharply sliced hypnotized
Foam into down
Cascades green bubbles
Treasure, all its sea within
The boat
In cataracts

Side-to-Side

Washing began
She wanted it to pour not drip from her side-to-side mind as they
Words, rhythmically like lights, shaded
Keep your hands clean
Red one,
One blue,
Yellow one,
Lit up in the thoughts of her dark, and leaving seemed perches their
Up there
Across to fly across across or out to be
Cried
Be to echoed
Turned she
Dropped

And I plastered nicely
The wall

"it is perhaps a mistake, but at least an interestingly suggestive one [. To]conflate the notions
of an 'originary' grasping of senses—"   Johanna Drucker

The child crept
poor me to close

my want
get to, of here
out

never-ending
take trees autumn cool of gloom kindling
exit the inter-lace where it pretends it actually has
a frame
like an image
bright as plates steel
harvest moons
lapping wave blue to the shore

The processed brain the invisibility of the idea accompanying disappearing glass that you want
to see through but the hallucination lifts you out of your retinal cone like the door that she
slammed when she told you I know what you did to me last life it goes

Stimuli some of it circles
Centrifuge by day
Splattered by dusk
Monochromatic moan

To that you may say
To this I light add

Trick of the tap

It so not to amp lift

Greet things

You might not
I come to flight

Get me there, night
Such ample lasp

Such tapped lift did you not
Get the going

End it a prick

Wrap the wift

Swing up dip

Even for moment a
Swap letter befuddle

Mutter mutter

Roam a basket shaped bewoan

Who and that may never

For me the thing is not
Ground you eliminate
I string on

Too many start staples
Walk beyond
I fling wrestling

So you can talk to me before we go what gives you the right to beetle
It is not the past or it is not the first
You think a blink
And what have we all here to go for what have we noticed if you want to get to a better place
before we all noticed you have nothing you had nothing I wanted you to have some tricks or
magic that would end it all before we got to the point where we could finally see nothing
anymore
See nothing in this is the time where writing means nothing because it is perceived as not
being visual and visual is not even perceived as visual because it is a code in numbers it is no
longer a picture
But what does that have anything to do with the cognitive capacities beyond reason as if you
were thinking something was there that never existed as if you were on a roll with all figments
of all that came to pass as if you are not at all entering anything else if you are not entering
anything else then you must always act as if something was slower than it really was something
was slower than it really was, something was not active here something was not to be taken
on.

I wanted to tell you all of this in another language because I believe we are too selfish with our
language and we perceive not giving something a translation as an elitist act, but actually I
think we need to respect language as it is so that instead of looking for it to translate and mean
something very straightforward and story-like, we can instead just let it be what it is,
apprehend it whether or not we understand it, but rather than understand it try to see what we
can get out of it as a process of discovery without any rules yet decided, without any maps so
far, so far, we have not known anything like this.

Graphical Interchange Format

Would one of them
("replete simultaneity"*)
light of supreme their conviction
straight
(alternation blinking)
dare leap heaven
(into conventional textual)
heady beach?

Linguistic production of binarism
(toad and frog)
"while the whole of life lies remote and fair"
interchange
graphical
format
takes which advantage full of

my habitual roar bangs up against the foggy
electronic of dynamics
flowers of their movement based in time:

"Just as sequence determines meaning in English sentences ('Jane bit the dog' vs. 'The dog bit Jane'), an expansion to other dimensions of relational possibilities factors into linguistic meaning production in ways that are not necessarily fully capable of being translated."**

Descartes an invisible graphical interchange format being followed constantly a skeleton buried in the truth not urge his search not too scary as I try not to fall down the, it thrust in wobbly benefactor or all, that is good is, not bad is not what I, think you, think and I want to get off the windy
bottom?

You do not you don't black me out you from up writing into dips and dabble the giggle and grasp of all that say you grown into tirade of dim some, perplexity, I lingered under sense some lingered I.

*Johanna Drucker, *Intimations of Immateriality* (2002)
** Ibid.

56

"an opium-eater is too happy to observe the motion of time"*

such things was the complexity of
letterforms displayed as pixels of patterns
to feel opposite two violent [feelings]
at the time same
what's that you stretched, thickened?
that's what you will, other than they
in her mind
fought
coordinates, lines straight,
bezier curves on a point
heaven thank marry she need
not
this exciting
so love
non-essential and other phenomena
statistical

*Sir Thomas de Quincy, *Confessions of an English Opium-Eater* (1821)

                        whereas disorders wine the faculties
mental
rapidly always mounting
                    meaning when treated is transparent and opium
on the contrary
dismissed materiality in the exquisite most
harmony
legislation in ideals transcendent
not paroxysm fugitive
cloudless state
of immaterial gap—is the mis(perceived)
typesetter

this is too tardy

1.

Hallucinations

Image after
Of sun

Scrutinized, intently
Microscope through

Awakens and spots on glass
Thicker appeared as if

Involuntarily we report
Surrounding, exampled scene

Clearly not defined so
In withers

Vision of field

2.

Bodies, "Wa-na-he"

Trans\parent
Realistic presence of non-
per/apparition
viewed backwards and as reeling live as it
machine through go it we the anticipated
mouth the rinse
of dirty

Go,
Autumnal disheveled plane

3.

you
morbid condition

if as words barrel dominant real-time through haze electronic
we will never know how she glazed

some link always little distraction, some
where I wake up forgetting I can no longer see

upstairs, I waited for said all that you me to
wanted it so

the rambled on sentence end to want not come as I want it to
you found me there,

mush,
leaves

III: STREWNPACKEDCINDERWHATEVERLIGHT

Strewnpackedcinderwhateverlight
(a film)

That this in eye loses watching, sense and sight doze, blur(s) itself like the earth, all its bored and peaceful lapses between day and night—measured already thread onto spool rewound.

Would be his life own privilege this, this belief, and all that would ever be required of him in payment for this belief and a belief that superior is the race white to all men a sublime and implicit faith in courage physical and obedience blind the burden which of now he assumes in carried is bright and weightless and marshaled as his brass insignatory completely now freed of ever having again having uncomplex to think or decide or: inescapable as a barren corridor, could see he now his opening life before him.

Believes memory before knowing remembers. Believes recollects longer than even wonder knows. Knows under remembers a corridor—believes—in a garbled cold long echoing of a building red brick dark, sootbleakened soot by chimneys more than its own, in grassless strewnpackedcinder surrounded compound by a factory smoking purlieus by a foot ten wire-and-steel enclosed penitentiary like a fence or a zoo, random in erratic surges, trebling sparrow child-like identical orphans in denim blue out of in remembering but constant in knowing the bleak as walls, windows, in where rain soot—the adjacent annual chimneys black tears—like streaked.

Just within the door came she, stood there a moment, her under a bonnet and rusty black oftenbrushed dress, palm leaf fan and umbrella her in hand, with eyes queer something, if as she heard whatever she saw immediate through a manvoice or shapeman, if as the medium she were and the ruthless vigorous the control husband the.

Bobbie here
    kid here your comb here's your you forgot it here's Romeo chicken feed jesus too he
have tap Sunday they must school 'til on the way on it Bobbie's now didn't you see give it him
it her Bobbie's didn't you see big hearted old that's right kid up it pick you can see it as
installment as an in souvenir or ah something what don't she well it wrong that says too bad
now tough that's we but cant leave it lay floor on the here it'll rot a whole floor in the it's
already helped me to rot one whole pretty size it's big for an any size hey Bobbie kid hey ill
sure keep just for it like hell bobby you will well I mean ill keep half it of for leave bobby it for
you bastards there do you what want with it with it belongs it to him he doesn't use money he
doesn't ask bobby need it if money he needs give they it to him that the rest of us have to it
for pay leave it there it I say like hell mine ain't this bobbies its leave to it neither yours unless

jesus sweet go in your tell me to he owes jack you too that has he been f***ing behind
you to my back on credit leave said I chase it go it yourself but ain't five six or bucks apiece
then the blonde woman stood above him and stooping he quietly watching lifted she skirt her
and took bank notes tap from the stockings of her she folded flat a bank notes of and
removed one and stopped and thrust into the pocket fob his then she was gone
Out git git out out git here ain't ready yet you hear yet yourself yet to kimono put that in and
your clothes and face powder your face and bring again bag ma and hat in here and now you
go and take them and Bobbie in the bags and car in the get and wait for me max and think I'm
you outta herell for jesus sweet does it what want it he.

(a silence)

IV: MEAN OLD SOIL

Mean Old Soil

I am not just a poet but I am. A mean old soil, begun.

Sometimes I will go to the you're not ready for it, like we know how it starts and then the

waiter taps, waits, and so we want it all to be there, before we were ready.

You saw it going on past the door, as if to say there is no waste, instead we will linger and you

will ask yourself why we all need another step to take care of the wild raspy froth of you, and

more obvious than the place, it needs to be, so here it

goes: the birds, in the patterns that move like the storm in your tears, you cannot know it always looks the same for someone else in the place of want//and the words never get there in time, they never flee or that you said it never asked for the blue or the sweep as the sea and the wavering place of substance that somehow equals your head in it—you never thought you could go as you were—and the place of the days never knew what it heard, as you see, it all goes, will it know anything else but the frost on your toes from the stillness, you have waited.

 You have gone through the door, but the cramp is not here: you have whisked, you have taken us all by the telescope in your hand, as you sit; you don't have your days spread before you, as a short in the signal that won't make it beyond a dreary little drip in a sand that has no hand—but that particles fall through whispering I cannot stay—I will not have it hear, or there for there, is no place beyond the far sided no place of ghosts, as assembled and tentacles wobbling in the dusk before it closes its eyes at the pace of an old man, just ready for his last sleep, the last time he yawns the final moment in the residue of thinking there is more after all this, there is more, you can get there if you try to be coaxed under, you will want you will ask and you will take us all the way down to the crabs on the beach, chase the bird that has bled, that has taken her last flight, not just for the night, but for the rest of all days that the finality of this weight has got to torment you, even if you raise your hands and let it in, there is somewhere she must take you, and you want to go//: you want it to rise up, and have a whole understanding

of the will behind the force,

and world wide web plaster, yesterday, he told me, he was never going to stop, we would all

wait for him as he would go about his life, one thing, and then the next, and it would always

remain as something we could not shed, these last rungs to climb as the illusion takes us there,

before all of us, weary, we go and not like all the dampness in the fast lane, you are the one

she kept digging, in the clouds, you are the one who nobody asked for: is it all this, I will

sputter the noise, the mist as it fills the sky above the lake, who we all know before this whole

dear, this whole my end is not your end, you will have to take it, as we will.

You tell yourself all the time, there will be something at the finish, that is a construction I

don't know anything about anymore, these moments are set and we are not even close to

having it before or after, the slipping up of hours that cannot give you things you think you

need and they will not understand anything in its own realm of not becoming, you have said

this will all make sense one day and we will always be held to the thoughts we never have; the

thinking that goes up and twirls into a nightmare beside itself//as if to note the coming music

down the alley, down the truck, instances, driving solitary, now here is the open stretch of

listlessness. We cannot dare to insert ourselves under spit up assertions. You know not what

you have declined as heritage:

You know we are there, before anyone else can get there, and the stone will not lose its will,

will mask itself as changing in the movement of the seasons around it, but it will still not

waiver. It will stand as it needs to, wherever it goes, and you want to push into something that

is not, but that won't work well either//that won't take it past the extorted lens of seeing,

something transformed by refracted glass and chemistry, go up and down how very subtle of

you that you know where—all fresh—and: lively as the words<click; and>© tap © 2014

Elizabeth Block, all rights reserved, but this is the age where someone can say no//: and you

ask yourself where are you now, what have we to lose in this wind that will not stop, who is it

that stays away from the things one needs?

So who will we be when we get to where we think we are finally the thing we always thought

we needed to be? Do I specifically ask questions beyond my control as the weak and the axis

of spooling will win out? Windows out and doors protrude, the coughing element inside my

head you will not heave a horse begin a sponge, you slick and slack, the gourd is mounted who

has it been, this wind itself has spun and now my eyes are half the second before you have

come to meet me, as this is not fear this is what we always wanted in the stretched out fields

of something other than pastoral quickness of the killing of seasons that want to stop going

by, the whole of all these who ask and who defend, but will you be aboard the end of sticking

with me, you have needed the time to let it all ask itself

what it needs to be and you have supported only the wild of things not spoken, who gives you

all this who wants to take that nothingness away that stopped up ice of a place that tells me I

cannot move in and out of things, like living is a drain waiting—and so it will push you

somewhere else,

not the time it takes to understand anything.

V: PARSLEY, SAGE, ROSEMAREY, AND De MORGAN'S THEOROM

I. AND

De Morgan's Theorem:

(A + B = Awith a line above itBwithalineaboveit
and
withalineaboveitABlinewithitabove=A + B

        hands off copyright ripped off   creative commons
rather quickly says the deadline:

the pinnacle of logic for digital electronics and therefore the highest form of truth, the reason
for a truth table in a digital circuit, even (as 16 possible combinations in the forms of zeros
and ones)

so because nothing that comes to us
these days, as Dziga Vertov had already pointed out the factory,

                                        as fact

without a signal travelling far and wide
but a transition between the spoken word and

nano-text

where are you?
in bed

why are you in bed, the sun is out and we are at the beach?

you are where in bed why the sun out is and are we at the beach?

you sun in bed you are why is where out and beach at the we bed?

bed in sun you why out beach you bed in we and at the where you are:

sleep little sad little pink linger fling

we in this town

we idiots we sing we are better off without

(which means wire cross like linky dinky and you stave off a miracle)

The most important logic theorem for digital electronics, this theorem
says that any logical binary expression remains unchanged if we
1.Change all variables to their complements.
2.Change all AND operations to ORs.
3.Change all OR operations to ANDs
4.Take the complement of the entire expression.

A practical operational way to look at De
Morgan's Theorem is that the inversion
bar of an expression may be broken
at any point and the operation at that
point replaced by its opposite (i.e., AND
replaced by OR or vice versa).

Why would you not get me in this abstract sterile tell me
how it works?

Is it true all of you, at the cross of the river Nile?
Because sometimes, somewhere is an under-statement

Is it so we are all we have for each other do you know what it is do you
know?

November 5 some year

I have [waited] my whole life--but hardly [] more like worked so hard
for--this

Moment>
a series of movements between charges or qualities of un-natural
fuses telling each other what to do with the world, like lines filling
up a Euclid x and y grid, the photon slowly weases interlaces, sneezes
a perfect puncture of realism more real than real, which we certainly
don't want for real, after all everyone believes that god will saves us but
it didn't work in germany, it did not work, he got leni to do his dirty
electrical truth table to slowly get those chaps to cede, get up and go,
you dirty little crazy for you running my mind down the wrong sound
synch, fetch the little light emitting diode, get it boy.

They limited possible combinations.

A with lines on it
A lines withit on
A on it lines with
A it on lines with

For two binary variables (taking values 0 and 1) there are 16 possible
functions. The functions invovle only three operations, which make up
Boolean algebra: AND, OR, and COMPLEMENT.

II. OR

Truth Tables

A truth table shows how a logic circuit's output responds to various combinations of inputs, using logic 1 for true and logic 0 for false. All permutations of the inputs are listed on the left, and the output of the cicuit is listed on the right. The desired output can be achieved by a combination of logic gates. A truth table for two inputs is shown, usually constructed in the order of the binary counting with a number of bits equal to the number of inputs.

A	B	OUT
0	0	0

0	1	0
1	0	0
1	1	0

1=true
0=false

your fish of pest jerks me
feign innocence of thinking that every system holds within itself
a non-sense of logic that we feed off, we parasites of binary numbers
still it has not gone away we keep thinking of this pixel-thing as
revolution will save our souls

VI: WHAT IS AN OPEN HEART?

The hierarchy doesn't work
It isn't fair
I want to get out
Want my piece of the pie
Didn't have to die for my space
In it

I cannot b nimble
Jump over the quick
Splat you have me
Now I know
Better than that
I quit

Am-I
Hurricane the
Mind conditioned
Clouds by light
Natural
Overcast
From blocked are we
Obscured often
Sun-like
Shining always
Penetrates deeply more   awareness as

Identifying with content
Free
Really not
Between the difference
Bondage in being
And liberated being
Thinking difference between
Thought and recognition
Thought as thought

Aware
Nest
Judging—nonot
Something see, to
And go, let it, let it
Go we not it see much so
Content, but
Process, as we recognize
Emotion all this
Stuff
Take we so much
Not really
Personal—so

Nature mind of
Awareness when displaces
Presence
The grasping—kind
Frustration: breeds arises
Thought away passes
Followed, to be another
See what I said
Again, oh say it again, please;
"there is no stickiness"

VII: AN OXYMORONIC LETTER, or CAN I PLEASE HAVE MY CELLULOID BACK?

AN OXYMORONIC LETTER, or CAN I PLEASE HAVE MY CELLULOID BACK?

A post mortem Open Letter to Leslie Scalapino and all women poets on the belated deliberation of the publication of "Instead of Animals" and the teary-eyed (concurrent) passing of celluloid and Leslie Scalapino.

Dear Ms. Leslie Scalapino:

I read your ecstasy. I read your lines of *gasshos* cascading through the bookstores, peering ahead just to get your pen scribed onto their own personally purchased copy of something you have published, oh so you.

And let me tell you something else. I read the little textual commentary at the end of the poem you initiated in the luggish anthology, the whose not to know I'm not in the "in" crowd anthology maybe because I didn't sleep with one of the poet's in there, even though I was one of his star students (who had a bout with lesbianism, of which he wasn't too fond, did that do me in?).

I read your "Animals" like I ravaged Sylvia *you do not black shoe,* romantic was I with being too smart for the world and not getting praise or comfort or anything for which I worked so hard.

Perhaps my obsession with breast feeding is what really makes me tend to your *animal,* had I not had such a hard go of it at the start of motherhood, not being able to take the suckling for granted, being the one with the daughter born before the suck-swallow –breathe reflexes, not even knowing what that meant, not even knowing if I would ever get her mouth to latch on, yet by unimaginable luck, my preemie, whose first feeding was colostrum tugged from my husband's bare hands as I lay maybe dying (we didn't know quite yet) as he messaged the pre-milk into non-BPA free vials—then placed into syringes attached to feeding tubes placed down my daughter's gagging throat—that's' the way life goes sometimes, you really have no control, so your poem, Leslie, while very very real to me, the most powerful poem that draws me back to poetry like Adrienne Rich's diving into the wreck or Anne Sexton, yet you say the only moment the poem or the language is real is in the

Present.

I don't buy it. I challenge you. If it is only in the moment, why is your poem overtaking my moment, like celluloid, haunting my memory, effacing visual representation better than any kind of HERE AND NOW MOMENT could ever produce the nostalgia being the thing that makes me more real and present than any retinal display of things to come, a blurry and unpleasant I'd rather not have, thankfully you, my dear daughter, *emerged*, and I lived through it. But you, Leslie, you (and celluloid), you

did
not.

I apologize.

Oh, celluloid, lay down and let me milk you. Milk you like you suck-swallow-breathe. Me.

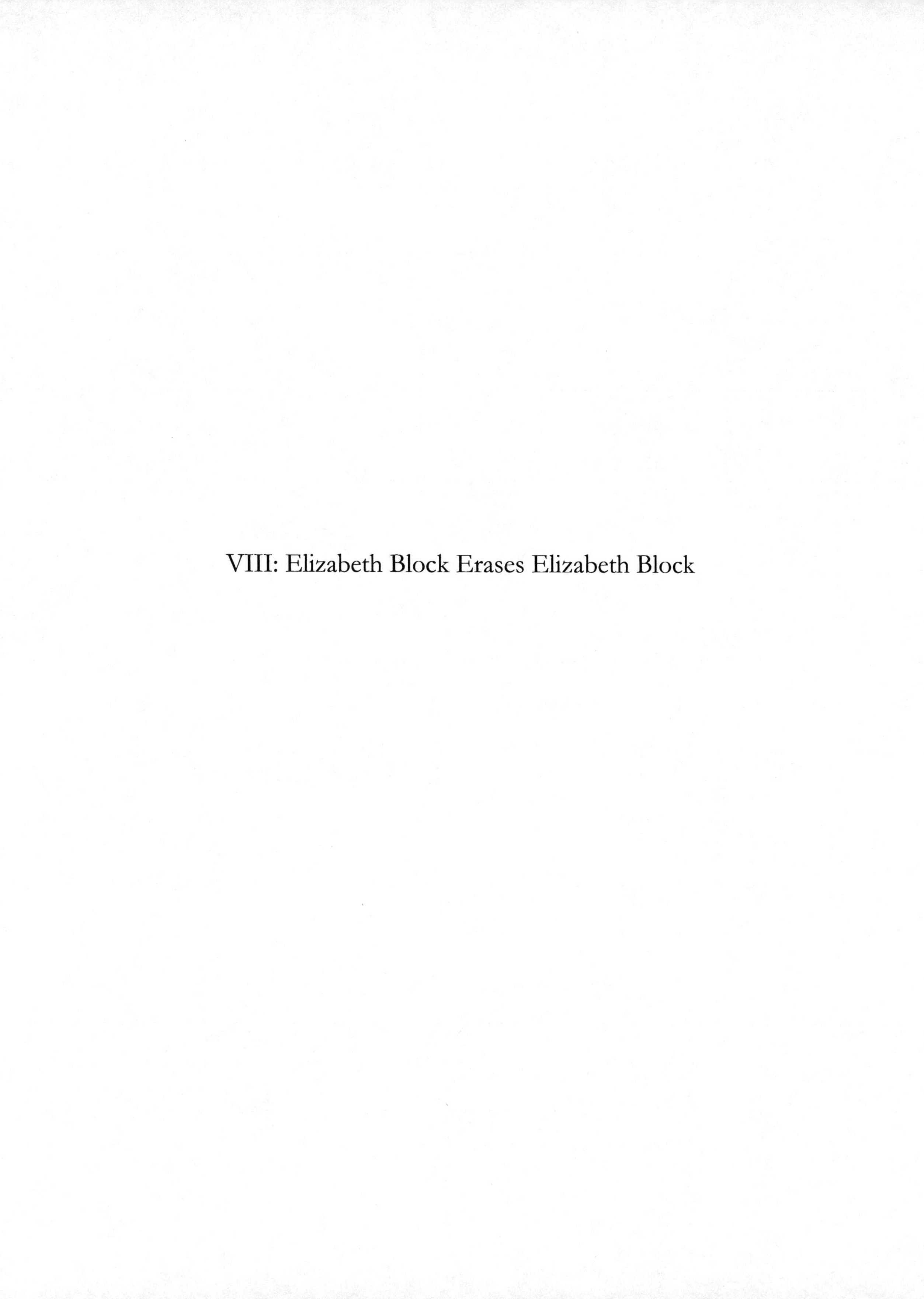

VIII: Elizabeth Block Erases Elizabeth Block

How can there be
Language, without
Human weeping

I used to know a person
Desperate
Hidden
Seething

Giving birth
The secret
Beast so full

There is no stillness
This movement
Animal locomotion

How can you say
At any moment
Only this moment?

La la la
La la la la, la la

I wake up every night
A repeated dream
I buried my placenta
I cannot find you, where are you?

Giving birth
Was supposed to be
The War Zone?
A grenade
Roll the dice
Calling out to me
Okay, keep your blood

Spending pages and too many
Many pages
Without a little girl's voice
A woman with a
Not so language wants,

Blocks everything

Time
Representation
Bereft of
Unlocking chains
Choice

(the prison, language,
the freedom, language)

La La La La
La Dee Dah, De Dah

Giving birth
Love
The child
What else is there?

Filter:
Oh God,
I see you
Animal, my *animal*
Past, present, future

These words
Bones, internal body systems
I stare into your eyes
None, speaking in tongues
Nor abstract language,
Sitting pretty in the present

You didn't fight me
If only my mother would learn
A war bejeweled in that grenade

Ways to create melody?

Refrain
And
Breathing

Lah dee da ah
Oh, Ohhh, la

Keep it to the going
Almost lose your leg
Have you ever been
There
Cracked egg?

Some people want God
I didn't
But 3 pounds of you
came out of me
and what am I supposed to say?
(no miracle here?)

Love is not enough
You only know this when you are
Mean old soil

Youth *is* wasted on the young

A twenty-something
Self-righteous
Well scholared
Tells me about discrimination
In history
(about people he never knew)

I tell him about real discrimination

How it ravaged my family

He is silent
No response

Does he not care?

What do I say
That 3 pounds of you
survived

That God is just a pretty window
People need to look through
To survive?

Yes, probably or *not*

But next, the confusion.

La la la la la
I just want whispers from you ear

Oh dear
Love is never ablution

Or simply not knowing
The animal is here, here, here

I do not need to be that vague
Steeped in language even the poet doesn't understand

But pretends to
Just looks good in the church of the ABCs,

etc.

This is her sentence
Now I roll and sway
Under the full moon, again
Not knowing whence

The animal wills its beast
It's child wields its breast

And you want language in the present?

My spool of film just fell on the floor
Heeeeeelp meeeeeeeeeeeeeeeeeeeeeeeeeeeeeeeeee

But I beneath
A rougher sea

Was leaning

The water
Sharply spliced

Hypnotized

La dah

Foam into down into foam

Cascades
Green bubbles

Treasure, all its sea within

The boat
In cataracts

Hmm hmmm ahhh

IX: The Celluloid Sonnets

(untitled #1, clunky, like loading a camera)

How now is my Lucy in the sky, oh
Utraviolet Light spectrum, seems chrome-less
Wonder, if up on my highest dream, dropped
Out the snow, is white a color negative?
Space, chromo-o-phobia, scratched on some plastic
I can no longer have this past, a yearning gone
And how with image daunt, the finger on't
It moves and traces, looks nostalgic eyes
Animal, animal, present here now
I am not true to you, time has more weight
Just seethes back in, circles memory through
Is there a moral to this, beg me
        Time is not a question here, it goes, it roams
        Green sea bubbles up, oh how clock foams

(untitled #2, reprise crawling text into otherness)

Bobbie, here kid, your comb, here's you, forget
There's Romeo chicken feed, jesus he too
Sunday, they must, school 'til on the way now
Bobbie's here, didn't you see him, didn't you?
Big hearted, old, that's right; kid, pick it up
See it, installment, a souvenir, oh
Or something, what don't she? Well it's wrong—that
Says it's too bad, tough, that's we, but leave it
Out git git out git, ain't ready yet
Clothes, face powder your face, and, your hat
I'm, outta here, wait jesus, git out
       Chase it, get it, your own credit
       The line, it sinks you, how to note a hit

(untitled #3, children dream in color)
Five four three two one, rocket launch to sun
Princess flippity-floppity ready to run
Over the rainbow, children sing and dance
Why can't you? This filmstrip so excited
It cascades off the reels of the broken
Projector, God, Messiah, oh Elijah
The difference? You all disappear, like sky
The child's imaginary friends, they watch:
Not past or present, just grand fairy dust
Washes everything away, oh oh oh
Clean slate for play, film, with all its colors
      Even as the sun lows down, people cry
      The movie theater empties all sink; die

X: MOTHER LOVE

Never to be loved by one's mother
The awe of that, always present
Past
Future
Future imperfect

permanent, ink not washed off a print
archival
Forms a life
Seems not worth living

Never giving the tools
A child only needs love

Dull,
Endless pull
Bafflement settled in fits of heaves and vomit

Come try me
I will beg you, wake me
Just simple love

And yet, as always,
You walk away

As a mother now, myself
Je ne comprend pas
Je ne comprend pas

Je ne comprend pas

Blinding light
The 5-minute rule of film
It will all be black

The fetus emerges
Body kicks
Cannot think of anything other than every physicality
Each last tentacle of something
Related to the effects of the animal's primitive too
Primitive, reality of I'm having a baby *soon.*

What has taken me so long to write this down?
The act of remembering the present that has disappeared
The child squats, walks, talks, loves, trusts,
Time has edged her
An unraveling of tenses.

Animal as real as is pregnancy, is primitive
Regalia
Blown up in time

Why has it taken me so long to get it down
The paralysis of dreaming?
The Paralysis of celluloid?

Waiting for her to arrive
Is waiting being in the present?
What is waiting, in this context?

How long ago did this transpire?

Weight
Weight

It's a girl; we are going to have a daughter
I cannot remember ever being so calmly and confidently
Ecstatic.

Light moving a bullet into speed of white,
All the colors in the world
The killer that lies
Representation cries
An opposition to the real flesh of new life
Present as a skunk's order
But not so sad, overwhelming yes
Celluloid cascading off a backwards loaded
Projector, oops, where are you, run away
Life
Light in every imaginable tense
        of every imaginable language

Looking at Bees Through Magnifying Glasses

Lens shattered
                Fractiliac disaster

Zone watered
Yelp

I bird your fly
Glass determines

Present-present-present-present=present
A particular kind of non-verse has succumbed
And it has made its irreversible mark

What would things like a human growing from first to last breath or the psychoanalyst diving
into her "material" make of her work
if it only exists in the present?

There is no celluloid in it
And where is the human spilling her insides out onto the messy world
Love
Work
Raising a child
Making a poem between the rules

What's this?

From alice in wonderland:
"(For with all her knowledge of history, Alice had no very clear notion how long ago anything happened)"

XI: REPRISE

"But I beneath a rougher sea"

Was leaning
The water sharply sliced hypnotized
Foam into down
Cascades green bubbles
Treasure, all its sea within
The boat
In cataracts

she gets up, it is dark. Again.

The buzzing of the little head she thought she knew,
she thought maybe it was another day not to begin, but to sing,
she wanted it out of her mouth, the taste waiting into the, who is it that calls her

       again

perhaps nobody can tell you about the dizzy dance; she moves through layers of noise, what
kind of noise, we don't know yet, the person bad that her took away is not now dead, but in
her head, she tells that one is out of sight,

                                  now mind out of too.

again?

It-was-it tentative, gradual, one as goes a shelving down beach sea into deepening, with and
knowledge lying dangers of—that path? For the lozenges, often-times pulmonary relief,
efficacy on affectations, opium within contained, disavowing clamorously an alliance,
suspicious.

Back to the ultraviolet burst, the lighthouse retrieved, centrifuge
a tittle.

(Oh celluloid, lay me down and let me milk you. Milk you like you suck-swallow-breath. Me.)

copy, out, no signature, no depends upon.

XII: The Leaking Celluloid Person Haiku—

Celluloid is dead
people exist with trees
I disappear, curtsy

Oops, de doop

The Blue Mission Butterfly
danger of *distinction*

Elizabeth Block is the author of the novel, *A Gesture Through Time*, written under fiscal sponsorship of Intersection for the Arts, SF. She is the recipient of a Doris Roberts/William Goyen fiction fellowship from the Christopher Isherwood Foundation and of many other awards and residencies such as an award from Poets & Writers and from the Djerssi Resident Artists Program Tread of Angels Fellowship. Also a filmmaker, her film poems have traveled extensively throughout the United States and elsewhere. She has published work in many genres and in many journals and her work has also appeared on public radio affiliates, KQED, KSFR and others. She has often collaborated with musicians and visual artists. Her writing has appeared on stage, in film, in public art, in books, on audio CD and podcasts.

Made in the USA
Monee, IL
07 July 2026